C000094963

How to survive
MARRIAGE

Clive Whichelow & Mike Haskins

Illustrations by Kate Rochester

summersdale

HOW TO SURVIVE MARRIAGE

Summersdale Publishers Ltd
46 West Street
Chichester
West Sussex
PO19 1RP
UK

www.summersdale.com

Printed and bound in China

ISBN: 978-1-84953-136-8

Substantial discounts on bulk quantities of Summersdale books are available to corporations, professional associations and other organisations. For details contact Summersdale Publishers by telephone: +44 (0) 1243 771107, fax: +44 (0) 1243 786300) or email: nicky@summersdale.com.

To Mum o Dad

love
From Karen o Colin
xxx

On your Golden
Wedding 2012,
guess you've got plenty of
your own survival tips !!

Other titles in this series:

INTRODUCTION

Marriage has its ups and downs — a bit like a white-knuckle ride, only slightly longer; and you can't get off and have a nice sit down when you feel like it.

The amazing thing is that when people embark on their life of wedded bliss they have no idea just how long it will last. They jump in feet first with blithe promises of 'for richer for poorer', 'in sickness and in health' and all that other stuff, little realising that this thing could last three times as long as their mortgage.

So what you need are survival skills.

The skills you need to survive marriage are probably greater than those needed for hacking your way through the undergrowth of an Amazonian jungle — blindfolded, and with only one leg. You need tenacity, staying power, and the patience of several saints — not to mention a sense of humour. Have fun!

THE GOOD NEWS

Somebody agreed to marry you – hurray!

There are now two people that think you're the most wonderful person that ever lived!

Together you're a world-beating team

REALITY CHECK

No one has ever been awarded a medal for surviving marriage, so don't expect a congratulatory letter from the Queen any time soon

If this was going to be easy they wouldn't bother making it legally binding!

It's very difficult to know if you made the right decision, as so far no one has invented an internet site called comparethemarriage.com

Have all the clichés about useless husbands, nagging wives and fearsome mothers-in-law told you nothing?

WEDDING DAY DISASTERS
TO AVOID

Trying to carry your partner over the
threshold and then using them as a
battering ram when you discover the
front door is stuck

Leading a conga out of the reception and not being able to find your way back

Insisting on taking your pets on the honeymoon

EMBRACE MARRIAGE WITH A GOOD DOSE OF IRONY

Keep a copy of your marriage vows on the fridge door

Cross off the days prison-style on the wall of your bedroom

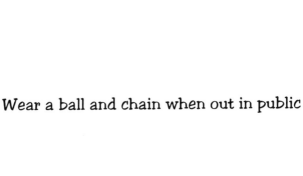

Wear a ball and chain when out in public

GOOD AND BAD
ROLE MODELS

Good	Bad
Couples who are always mutually supportive	Couples who like nothing better than to tell complete strangers all their partner's worst faults in great detail
Couples who are at ease with each other's opinions	Couples who start looking up divorce lawyers if either of them so much as criticises the other's music collection
Couples who've kept the romance alive by meeting their partner's needs	People who've kept the romance alive by meeting other partners
Couples who enjoy the benefits of a family life	Couples who enjoy the life of a family on benefits

REMEMBER – THIS ISN'T A TRIAL RUN!

Your wedding day is the most wonderful, perfect day in your partner's life – so just make sure what follows doesn't seem like an anticlimax!

You both have to love, honour and obey – you can't just do one of these jobs and leave the others for your partner!

You can't get away with signing the
marriage register in pencil

If, however, you eventually decide your
marriage has been a trial run, don't
mention this fact when telling your
partner you want a divorce

BASIC LESSONS TO
REMEMBER

If you were looking for a loving, loyal and
unquestioning companion you should
probably have got a spaniel instead

Telling your partner how attractive they
look will get you far — just as long as
you're not ogling someone else when you
say it

The person you have married is your life partner, not your life sentence!

REALISTIC AND UNREALISTIC GOALS FOR YOUR MARRIAGE

Realistic: Finding someone who shares your interests

Unrealistic: Finding someone who will share all the debts you've clocked up over the years

Realistic: Having children you can be proud of

Unrealistic: Having children who become billionaires and keep you in the lap of luxury forever

Realistic: Building a home together just the way you want it

Unrealistic: Building separate homes for each of you just the way you want them

TYPES OF MARRIAGE PARTNER YOU COULD BE

Domineering — why stop here, why not just take over a small country?

An assertive equal — but some are more equal than others, right?

Submissive – don't cave in, demand a new pinny every now and then!

The innocent bystander – just stand back and let your super-confident partner sort out every problem. A lifetime of amusement will surely follow!

The passionate partner – the sort who is overcome with desire whenever they see their spouse. If you can keep this up when you're both in your nineties, congratulations!

SCIENCE AND NON-SCIENCE

It only takes 13 muscles to smile, but 47 to frown — boy, is your face in for some exercise!

In finding a mate for life you are now in the company of apes, vultures and pigeons — but should we judge you by the company you keep?

Married people tend to have bigger waistlines than single people — maybe they always feel the need to take the last biscuit in the jar before their partner nabs it

A high percentage of marriages end if the husband or wife faces trial for murder. If the murder in question is that of their partner, the percentage is even higher

According to one survey the average married couple spends just four minutes alone together each day — that's only a little over 24 hours per year!

READY RESPONSES FOR THINGS OTHERS WILL SAY TO YOU

'Will we be hearing the pitter-patter of tiny feet soon?'

'Why? Do you have mice?'

'Don't forget to let your partner know who's boss!'

'I tried but it turned out the vacancy had already been filled'

'There's no getting out of it now!'
'That's what they said to Houdini!'

'You're bound to have your ups
and downs'
'Yes, my blood pressure's going up and
my bank balance is going down'

INADVISABLE WAYS OF SAVING TIME AND MONEY

Asking the vicar if he'll do a 'buy one get one free' deal on the wedding service

Drawing up a rota for which of you will wash the dishes to cover every mealtime for the entire duration of your marriage

Having the children a few years in advance so they can be bridesmaids and pageboys

DOS AND DON'TS

Do make your partner tea in
bed occasionally

Don't get ambitious and try a
barbecue, though

Do write your partner little love poems

Don't make them limericks about young
ladies from Bude or old men from Kent

Do show genuine interest in what your partner does

Don't do this by hiring a private detective to follow them wherever they go

MOMENTS YOU MAY HAVE TO CONTROL YOUR TEMPER

When you find a bag of your favourite clothes put out for a charity collection

When you find your partner has emptied your joint bank account three weeks before payday

When your partner returns from the shops with a present for themselves and nothing for you

When your spouse buys you a crash diet
book for your birthday

When your partner comments on the state
of the bedroom ceiling during lovemaking

SELF-HELP BOOKS YOU MIGHT WANT TO READ

How to Bite Your Tongue Under
Extreme Provocation

How to Speak 'Apologese'

How to Stop Nagging in Fourteen Days

1,001 Compliments You Can Give Your Partner Without Making Them Think You're After Something

How to Stay in Shape Without Your Partner Thinking You're Having an Affair

HOW TO MAINTAIN WEDDED BLISS

Not only have you got someone with
whom you can enjoy all life has to offer,
you can take it in turns to do
the housework!

Go away for a weekend and sign in at the
hotel as Mr & Mrs Smith (unless you are
Mr & Mrs Smith of course!)

Get all dressed up for an evening out, then stay in!

FANTASIES YOU MAY START HAVING

You are married to the most famous person in the world but they look, act and sound just like your real life partner

You are an actor in a continuous TV ad break for homecare products

All your neighbours and your partner's friends are secretly lusting after you

You wake up in the aisle of the church after fainting and have time to reconsider

You are a pet animal owned by
your partner

DON'T TRY TO LIVE UP TO AN IMPOSSIBLE IDEAL

Who wants a fairytale wedding – have you actually tried walking in glass slippers?

You don't have to be a superhero all the time – though it's useful every so often

To have a marriage made in heaven you have to be dead first

STARTLING STATS

By 2010 Herbert and Zelmyra Fisher of
North Carolina, USA had been married for
86 years

So that's 85 years, 11 months, 27 days
and 17 hours longer than Britney Spears'
first marriage!

A woman from Indiana, USA holds the Guinness World Record for being married the most times. In 2009 she was considering her twenty-fourth marriage because 'it gets lonely'

Presumably because her 23 previous husbands were out of the house all the time having formed two complete football teams plus referee

CHANGES THAT WILL HAPPEN TO YOUR APPEARANCE

Husbands will become better-dressed
following marriage

Wives will dress more casually, although
their wardrobes will still mysteriously fill
with the latest fashions

After a while you may find you have started dressing in matching outfits (and possibly matching underwear, too)

Wives cut down on the slap and husbands
cut down on the tickle

Once your partner has seen you first
thing in the morning, anything goes!

TRY NOT TO THINK ABOUT THE COST OF THE WEDDING

You could have gone on the holiday of a lifetime. But then when you got back you'd have had no money left to marry the love of your life!

You could have bought the entire contents of your local pound shop and kitted out your house — or started your own pound shop!

For the same price you paid for your wedding you could have bought a new car! But at least now you'll have someone to ride on your tandem with you!

With that amount of money you could have taken a few months off work! But there'd have been no one at home to make it worthwhile!

You could have bought several thousand lottery tickets and maybe lived the rest of your life in luxury (or possibly penury)

ADVICE YOU WILL GET FROM OTHERS (AND CAN SAFELY IGNORE)

'Never have any secrets from one another'

'The secret of a long marriage is to spend as little time together as possible!'

'Once you're married, you don't have to buy presents for each other any more!'

'Make sure you get a joint bank account'

'Don't go and ruin it by having kids'

'Who needs money when you're in love?'

DO SOMETHING MARRIED COUPLES ARE SUPPOSED TO DO

Share a bath occasionally — but not with your entire Sunday league football team

Look genuinely pleased to see each other
– but not every time you're passing on
the stairs

Hold hands in public – but not
when swimming

Actually have a conversation when out for a drink — but perhaps a bit more of an interesting one than 'Whose round is it, then?'

Have a slow dance together at a party — and not just when you're drunk!

KEEP THE ROMANCE ALIVE

Romantic weekends away – just make sure it's with your partner though

Treat your partner to a sensuous massage – but avoid slapping them and timing how long it takes for the ripples to subside

Pay compliments to each other — but not
along the lines of 'Your grouting
is amazing'

Dine by candlelight — but resist the
opportunity to comment on how much
electricity you're saving

Cuddle – although maybe not while either
of you is driving

TRICKS TO MAKE OTHERS THINK YOU KNOW WHAT YOU ARE DOING

Become an adviser at Relate

Bulk-buy anniversary gifts and cards for the next few years

If anyone asks you 'How's married life?'
respond with immediate enthusiasm
rather than looking pained and confused
for several moments

Close all the windows and doors and make
sure no one is passing by before having a
row with each other

Perfect your 'jolly married couple' comedy double act routine which the pair of you can immediately go into at any social gatherings

ARGUMENTS YOU MAY FIND YOURSELF FALLING INTO

'I should have listened to what my mother said about you...!'

'You know you're lucky you're married to someone as patient as I am!'

'Well it's the way I always did it before I was married and it worked perfectly well!'

'I didn't know you were taking those marriage vows literally!'

THINGS YOU'LL FIND YOURSELF WORRYING ABOUT

Unimportant: The fact that you and your partner have started to look and act alike

Important: You wake up to find that you have actually become your partner

Unimportant: Whether people will assume that your pet dog/cat is a child substitute

Important: Your partner is dressing the dog/cat up in a romper suit

Unimportant: Whether your snoring is a valid reason for your partner to seek a divorce

Important: Whether your partner's snoring will keep you awake for the rest of the marriage

THINK POSITIVELY

Someone will actually be putting up with
you for all those years!

Once you're married you'll never be stuck
for something to do – or for someone to
tell you to do it

Who else would tolerate your foul moods, disgusting habits and inability to remember anything?

www.summersdale.com